## About the Author

A retired United Reformed Church minister now living in Dorset. Ann's background is as a Speech and Drama teacher and as a counsellor and psychotherapist. She spent many years working in hospitals, centres and schools and was for thirteen years an external examiner for the London College of Music and Media.

# Love Your Memories -- To Begin

**Ann G. McNair**

Love Your Memories -- To Begin

Olympia Publishers
*London*

**www.olympiapublishers.com**
OLYMPIA PAPERBACK EDITION

A CIP catalogue record for this title is
available from the British Library.

ISBN: 978-1-80074-846-0

First Published in 2023

Olympia Publishers
Tallis House
2 Tallis Street
London
EC4Y 0AB

Printed in Great Britain

## Dedication

I dedicate this book to Linda and David, my two surviving children.

# Love Your Memories – To Begin

It seems that the whole of life is about remembering and forgetting. Bringing to life the things that uplift and generate good feelings, and allowing the mind to push away for a time the things that make for a state of unhappiness. Then depending how we wish to feel at a particular moment we select one or the other.

How simple it all seems, when we think in those terms. Recognising we can take the initiative and make things better. It's when that initiative has been hampered by undesirable interventions that things appear less straight forward.

I'm not writing a textbook on psychotherapy even if I was capable of it, but by bringing to life some of the things for good in my own life, I might possibly enkindle a spark of positive thought in another's.

Oh to be free of all care
To be keen with a zip
As the nip in the air.
To be gay, to be sad, to be lost, all unseen
And uncalled from the nymph of the flare.

To linger in heights

9

With the moon and the stars
Hear a train rumble softly below
And see mile upon mile
Of lights from small cars
Silent passengers move to and fro.

What is the key note
To rest in such bliss?
Enough close encounters
Can settle the score
And for minutes we're free
To respond to the muse
With pure energy flowing once more.

# Love Your Memories – Two

It is at times remarkable, how one thing leads to another, which for me meant an opportunity to continue developing my work as a drama therapist. After hearing of the work I had been doing for a number of years with satisfactory results, then seeing me work, I was accepted for the post. There were regular meetings with those in charge and of course a certain amount of monitoring from week to week, though I was mainly left to my own devices, so I guess I was trusted and able to build the sessions as I felt appropriate.

The appointment was for one session a week in the psychiatric unit of a London hospital, working as a 'mind and drama' therapist.

At the start of each session, unless there was vital information I needed to know about these very vulnerable people (they were all in-patients at the time), my choice, was to know as little as possible about them.

After a few minutes into a session, one could sense the overall feelings in the room, and after a friendly introduction by me, someone invariably spoke.

Being deeply aware of the impact that someone like myself as a stranger coming into their safe place might have, I was extra careful. Much of my work was about listening, picking up on feelings individually and corporately and each week, acknowledging in whatever way was appropriate, those who were still in-patients, as some may have been discharged during the week, while making the necessary adjustment to include any new people who had come into the group.

Some weeks the atmosphere was lifted by using conducted fantasies, that is, by leading the patients through a story-line with an inspiring end in view; often with background music and watching to see if the ideas were acceptable and how each appeared to respond to what they were being asked to think about.
There were times when each could choose at that moment where their ideal place might be. I gave four ideas;

1.In a log cabin on a mountain - top sitting in front of a roaring fire;
2. Sitting on a deck chair in a warm location with the sound of the sea lapping the shore;
3.Walking over hills on a spring morning with a fresh breeze and the sun on their back; or
4.Sitting in a beautiful garden having tea with friends, or just sitting comfortably, drinking in the sounds and scent of the flowers and preparing to fall asleep.

Mostly one or other of these suggestions found a comfortable place in the group.

On one occasion, with very dramatic music, which I had carefully prepared beforehand, I was conducting the group through a blizzard. One gentleman in particular fully participated with such realistic movements, that the others were almost in awe of him and gradually left him to it. The experience proved to be life-changing as through his tears he was saying thank you to what appeared to be his God for helping him to re-live a war-time experience which had left him exhausted but free at last. He had emerged unhurt and all the fear and agony had wafted away. I understand he made a fairly rapid recovery afterwards.

Some days we might be making imaginary phone-calls in turn, with each person being able to own his or her secret communication without having to share what it was that allowed them to feel in charge, at this point. The group usually wanted to share, and many things were disclosed very willingly which all added to individual feelings of well-being. It was similar with writing imaginary letters where faces would express an aim of one sort or another. Each person was given a space and time to improvise their choice of communication.
As they got to know me, most of the group opened up to speak of some of the things that had brought them so low. Much was gained from imagining something that was in the way of their life or their recovery, and so we might symbolise that thing as a locked door or a drawer perhaps, and depending on the intensity of the feeling, the obstacle could vary accordingly; they might imagine trying to remove it, or say how it might be removed with help, and indeed the sort of help needed in their estimation to get the job done.

In the middle of one session, a gentleman clearly was finding it necessary to shout out the fact that he wished he had never been born. He indicated what he thought of the session, something which he said, was of no help to him. His wish he said was just to blot out the whole of his past life as though he had never been born. He would not be reasoned with, and persisted in declaring he still wished he had never been born. I said he could have his wish here and directed the others to imagine the same. The session was about important times in their lives, anything they remembered which brought back treasured moments. The gentleman kept trying to speak, but I reminded him of his wish and what that would entail. Eventually he could see that there was so much in his life to love and look back on, and for the time-being he would like to be back in the group.

Poetry for most was interesting and beneficial. One gentleman suddenly began reciting poems from Tennyson, a particular favourite of his. Afterwards he told us that his mother used to recite many of this poet's works to him which he loved to remember. I remembered one school prize I had which was the works of Tennyson. He no longer had the book that had belonged to his mother. I brought my copy in the following week and presented it to him. He was quite overcome and could not believe that he was meant to keep it, but when he eventually accepted it, there was great delight on his face. It was like giving him back a part of his mother to cherish once again.

I continued to encourage everyone to share their talents and skills whenever possible and of course their unique experiences in war and peace.

One day I met a lady as I was going in to lead the session. I recognised her as a former patient. She started to laugh loudly on seeing me, and recounted how hostile she had been to me. How she had thought me mad at the time, but had later realised it was all for the good, and she took it for granted we were now good friends. I assured her that we were, and we shook hands.

We were all very sad when the Hospital authorities informed us that there was no longer the finance to continue with the sessions.
I led these weekly sessions there for a number of years in the 1970s and the work carried out, not just by myself – for I learned there were sessions going on in art, craft and gardening which were wonderful outlets for the many people who passed through these doors and for those of us who genuinely tried to make a difference where there was a need

I feel privileged and greatly blessed to have been a part of it all.

# Love Your Memories - Three

Have you ever wondered why certain objects or pieces of clothing have certain significances or attraction for you, and know that somewhere in memory there is a story to tell which could explain and in some cases modify, what appears to be an almost strange attraction, when the eyes are drawn to, perhaps even fixed on what we see.

**In my case, I have identified three things** at present which have continued to be of considerable importance to me, in my way of thinking.

# The First Is a Pretty Pale Blue Party Dress

I had been staying with my mother in a convalescent home in Kilmun where she was recovering from a big operation. It was right at the beginning of the war and although Dad had been given forty-eight hours' compassionate leave, Mother was still in hospital when he had to leave. It's only when one is older that the true significance of such a parting comes home.

It was nearing my fourth birthday. My older sister was staying with Grandma and my brother who was much older was already working at home and at the age of fifteen, was being looked after by a friend – although I imagine thinking he could look after himself. Mother was growing stronger each day and now able to take short walks around this little seaside town.

The ladies in the home were all very kind and frequently gave me pennies which I put into a little tartan purse Mum had bought for me. One day someone actually gave me a shilling, although I offered that to help pay for breakages, when feeling a little tired, (the ladies seemed to be talking for a long time), I sat on a low shelf of the shop where we had stopped and knocked over a number of glasses and afterwards I tried to make sure wherever I sat was safe. Quite a lot of money especially for a small child.

Mother always took me with her of course but this day she said I should have my hair cut, and because she needed to look round the shops, perhaps I could stay with the very nice ladies in the hairdressers while she and a friend she had met in the home quickly disappeared for a short time. What would I like her to bring me back as a gift? I had this thing about building blocks, as I had seen the children playing with them at school when we had on occasion been in a classroom where my sister happened to be. I didn't realise it was my fourth birthday and mother had planned a little celebration that evening. I didn't cry, feeling sure she wouldn't leave me there forever and with the picture of building blocks in my mind, that I hoped she was able to find, I was almost at ease.

She couldn't find any building blocks but brought me a cloth doll with a curly knob of hair on her forehead. I confess to being disappointed although it was a nice doll. Now I could give her a haircut as I had watched the ladies doing earlier. I was feeling rather pleased with my efforts until I realised her hair wouldn't grow again and had a little cry.

Later my mother unwrapped the pale blue party dress which was a delight and a perfect fit. I twirled around and laughed and was very excited and admired myself in the mirror until a little cake was produced with some of the ladies there to add to the joy of the occasion.

The particular lady my mother had befriended had an unusual name, so it was one that stuck in my memory. It was Mrs Butterfly. Many of the ladies were quite ill and wouldn't live for very long. My mother's friend was one of them.

The dress, I kept long after I had outgrown it until one day a lady who was quite well known to the neighbourhood who we helped out (with some outgrown clothes which she could sell or use for her family), as I was told she was very poor, came with a particular need and out came my little blue dress. I was persuaded her child's need was greater, and mother asking, of what use was the dress to me now. The lady insisted I take sixpence which almost made the parting worse, but to me ever after the memory of the blue dress has been special.

# The Second Is the Ring

The ring, with the large pale blue stone set in silver.
Special? Yes, because of the story behind it.
When Great Uncle George went out to Canada at the time
of "The gold rush," he didn't find too much gold but a fair
amount of silver, and had a ring fashioned for his wife
with a stone found in the area.
Some years later, the store which Uncle George and his
wife Mary ran together, caught fire one night and being
mainly of a wooden construction, burned to the ground.
Uncle George only just survived, but sadly his beloved
wife did not.
One can only imagine the trauma he went through at the
time, taking its toll on George emotionally as well as
physically (for he lost part of a lung as a result).
Many years later, when George was able to visit family in
Scotland, the precious ring which he had kept, was passed
down to his sister Katherine, my mother-in-law, and one
day to me.
I felt very honoured to be given such a gift, and set out to
find out what stone it was.
The first jeweller took one look at it and said he thought it
was glass. I reasoned in my head, knowing the story
behind it, that he was mistaken.
The next jeweller was able to test it, and quickly
determined that it certainly was not glass. It seems

plausible that because it was set in silver and not gold and was such a large stone as well, sensible to think it was glass.

Within a very short time, this jeweller had identified the stone which he told me was very hard, though not quite as hard as a diamond, and was called Cancrinite, usually found in parts of Canada, though not usually blue, but rather yellow or a variant of that in colour.

I asked if anything might have happened to have changed its colour, and he said immediately 'intense heat.'

I have since discovered that it was found in a variety of colours in different parts, but I was told that blue would have been quite rare in the Yukon.

# Great Uncle George

Great Uncle George could wiggle his ears.
He looked quite like Dad
Rather Dad looked like him
He left Scotland for the gold Rush
But developed TB
From the hardships he bore
Lost a lung but stayed strong
He recovered and more
Worked so hard for years
And opened a store
For a long time was happy
With his wife by his side
Well loved by all
And a small sense of pride
But one night a fire
Destroyed all that they had
And tragically too, his dear wife died.
He found some new work
With a Canadian firm
And worked his way up
And stayed there long term.
When at last he retired
Now with just half a lung
Made more trips to his homeland
To see those he held dear

Sisters and nephews, great nephews and nieces
Where they found him unchanged –
Though now not so strong
But through laughter and tears
For the children he loved
He still wiggled his ears.
And gave thanks up above.

# The Third Bangles

I seemed to have a fascination for, from a very early age, bangles.

Whether it was a thought that they had some protective qualities which would cover my somewhat vulnerable, as I imagined, wrists; I couldn't have chosen more unsuitable objects. If it was round and would slip over my hand and was tight enough to stay on, I was content. Many a time mother had to persuade me to let go of the latest fancy and understand the discomforts and even the danger of cutting myself that they presented.

Whether our neighbours heard of this or not I can't be sure, but one day they very kindly presented me with a beautiful gold flat rope bangle which I wore virtually every day.

So great was my attachment that I was still wearing it when I went to secondary school. By this time it was beginning to become a little too tight, so I decided to heed the family's advice and have it removed.

I chose to ask our wonderful science teacher, if he could help and he quickly cut through the metal. It was evident to him immediately that it wasn't gold but it still looked splendid, and he very softly informed me of his findings, and being a science teacher told my how he knew. A helping hand and a science lesson all in one.

Many times afterwards through the years, my eyes have been drawn to bangles comparing them to THE ONE but never found one like it.
The nearest I have come to it was when we were on holiday in Hungary. Once I tried it on, I was captured by it and happily left the shop with my precious parcel safely in my bag.

I have since connected this strange attraction to an early incident in my life, when I was burned on the wrists through being dared to come too close to a hot iron, and of course being a very young child, did just that. I should add, it happened while my mother was in hospital. In such circumstances, I think I was making a statement.

It is only after many, many years that I was able to compose this well-remembered incident, for fear of tarnishing my wonderful mother's memory.

# THE STRAW HAT

I don't have to hurry,
I'm not going to hurry
I haven't done anything wrong,
Though mother has worked herself into a state
And by all accounts we are going to be late
What could be so terribly wrong?
I just want to burst into song.

The hat on my head,
Already feels tight.
I just want the feel of the sun and the sand,
And a paddle would feel so terrible grand.
Not a head that is bursting so tightly confined
No matter how lovely the ribbons that bind
The straw to my head, she may think in her mind
Are perfectly right for today.

I may have been ill
But my goodness I'm well

I can run, I feel good, my breathing can tell
I don't need to go back to bed.
But attempts to feel free with sea breeze in my hair
Have been thwarted by Mother who's in some despair
To keep this straw hat on my head.

At last she gave in with a terrible frown,
And in some distress she had to sit down
With a warning that I could get ill once again
If only I'd listen to her wise decision
And that it was worth some discomfort and pain
To keep the straw hat on my head.

# Full Memory Recall of a Particular Day in Childhood

It is summer and I am five years old.
A warm cloak of sun lulls me in the hot afternoon.
The grass smells sweet, the ramblers
beautiful; their scented petals made secret perfume for me
that very day, as though the life within them was
crying out for recognition and I the only one who knew.

The war seems very far away, as I pick
more daisies. A good garden shouldn't have any anyway,
So Jimmy next door says, and he's always right and so
clever. He would have been a surgeon his mother says –
I don't know why he isn't – he does make
beautiful pancakes.
I remember the day he came round with two,
Iced clearly with Isobel and Ann – but
he never did give me back my stick
He said he'd painted to keep me from getting splinters.

I wonder if Daddy will come today?
Mummy said something to somebody that he might.
I think she was frightened in case we got excited and he
didn't come after all.
Perhaps I'll look up and through my funny wet eyelashes,

Besides the pretty patterns that the sun makes
When I blink slowly?
I'll see my Daddy striding towards me
looking like someone else in his uniform.
I know, I'll give him a surprise.
I'll cut the grass with the scissors, and it does need
cutting and he'll walk right past and not know the house
because the garden will look so different,
and I'll laugh and call out, 'It's ME!'

Fortuitous or providential? Those moments when our attention is arrested in time to save what could have been a serious outcome?

# FRIENDS

I was washing the car with a bucket and sponge,
No other sound could be heard.
I was trying to be quick to get on with my day
And the tasks I much preferred.

Half way through I stopped to hear
The sudden chirp of a bird
As though it was sending a message?
Though no sign or movement was heard.

As I lifted the sponge straight way to my side
Came a little feathered friend,
Again he chirped and made me turn
I paused a moment and then

I realised that with one more step
Like pussy in the well
I'd have fallen into the water
With what bruising who can tell?

The bird stood close and unafraid,
With his head turned up to the sun,
How I thanked the little creature,
For the wonderful thing he had done.

We acknowledged one another
I was saved from imaginings feared,
And as I turned to see how close
He quietly disappeared.

I was deeply moved to write –


# ON SEEING THE FILM "THE BOY IN THE STRIPED PYJAMAS"


Not of his making the close confines
In contrast to loving freedom in meadow or farm
Not so today while adult family take pains to hide or
confuse
What no-one seems to know is taking place,
Within walking distance of that garden
behind the house. A house so buttoned up–
A dying house with fearful servants and guards
Who spy or talk too much then disappear, to be seen no
more.
Like a little boy who broke out to explore the forbidden
ground Seeking a kindred soul and finding a boy his age in
striped pyjamas–
Shorn and pale with empty stomach but childlike spirit.
They grow to absorb each other's place and
Dream of different times
When wire is trodden down; but for now one will
Cross to find a father lost,

Only way was under – spade bursting through to reach a
friend.
Hand in hand now through the rain, siren howls
And two small figures are hurled in to the chamber with
Crowds of the unwanted dying,
Thoughts closeted in trust of showers to warm them from
the rain.
Only a black mist like coal dust through the little chink of
sky
To take their breath away in wonder and strange
excitement
Or fear; hands tightly clasped together, doused to fall
asleep.

How often have you met someone who maintains they have no interest whatsoever in poetry, and will not give an opportunity to anyone to prove them wrong.

The number of times I have said to someone that there is poetry for everyone and if they don't find one that moves them, makes them laugh or makes them think, they are missing out on much pleasure and enjoyment in their lives. The following poem I wrote with partly this in mind, but mainly for the sheer fun of conveying a possible idea and scenario which could well be true without offending or degrading a single soul.

# Love Your Memories - A Cornflake

## THE MAN WITH THE CORNFLAKE STUCK TO HIS FACE

A man with a cornflake stuck to his face,
Knew his wife thought it some kind of disgrace;
Though how it had come there
Was not in contention
That it splashed during breakfast
Is scarce worth the mention:
But he'd had enough of being told what to do and
What's wrong with your foot?
You're not walking quite right.
Do you need bigger shoes?
Are your laces too tight?
He answered the door with a man standing there
Who thought that the owner was quite unaware
Of the cornflake though stuck should have been no
disgrace
But seemed quite comfortably stuck to his face.
The caller not meaning offence or distaste
With a trembling finger mirror imaged the place
To the man with the cornflake stuck to his face.
What do you want? roared the man of the house.

The caller so sorry for disturbing his day
Said I'll call again later if you say that I may?
You're here now, what is it? said the man of the house
I'm selling wood glue said the man at the door
In a voice of a whisper, I've been here before.
Oh yes, then we'll have some was the angry reply.
Three pots should do it, is it easy to apply?
It depends what you're sticking? said the man with a cry,
A roar of forced laughter meant stop, enough said,
Do you think it might keep me from losing my head?
With some little effort, he opened a pot,
Loudly read out instructions to show what was what.
As he swished off a fly the flake loosened and flew,
Not on top of the pot,
But inside with the glue.

# Love Your Memories - Granny

So many clear recollections that can only be told in
poems, as when
someone very dear is no longer around. My great
grandmother
affectionally known to us as Granny, died when I was six
and had a profound effect on me as I have recalled in my
poem

# FINDING OUT

'I want to see Granny'
I knew that she was dead,
Now in the front parlour,
Not resting in her bed.

They try to keep me out,
And I cannot think why,
But I keep on asking
For I want to say goodbye.

Now I'm getting more upset
So at last they let me in
With a promise not to cry
As though it were a sin.

For me it was so special,
Though only six years old,
The sun shone in upon her face
She didn't look so old.

'Isn't she lovely?' the words spilled out
I felt her warm caress,
All that she meant was with me still
Just sent from a different address.

# POST 1945

After the Second World War, even ordinary scenes of everyday life like the following, often helped us to appreciate what we had, and for some, like myself, still just a child, added a gentle feeling of security.

# WHO'D HAVE THOUGHT

We'd just been to the dairy,
To buy a loaf of bread.
'It's just two slices per head today,
Post-war rationing,' they said.

Still when farming gets back to normal,
And we're growing a better crop,
There'll soon be bread aplenty,
We're told in our local shop.

But for now it's strictest rationing,
Who'd have thought it would come to this.
Bain the baker wanted to give us more
But he couldn't take the risk.

He knew the number of customers
His bread must feed each day.
Exactly the number of slices
In each loaf, it's true to say.

Of course other things were rationed
Up till 1953.
But to ration our staple diet
We never thought to see.

There weren't all the substitutes
And money was tight they said.
Even in the short time it lasted,
We just longed for a loaf of bread.

# Love Your Memories - Pearl

My first little friend I can remember, and one I persuaded to come to the Junior Church Choir with me at the age of seven was Marilyn.

It was not something she enjoyed, but as she was going to move away soon after to London, it would have been one less thing to fret over and leave behind.

# PEARL

Going away Marilyn?
With your golden curls
And cheeks like peach bloom
And gentle nature of my little friend.
What are you seven or eight? You
Seem younger in the memory.
Hope you will be happy in that big place
Where the Queen lives.

Coming back Marilyn?
Now twelve years old like me;
To the same street
With the same friends to follow
You out along the Lambhill Road
To the newest little grave.
Your own wish, to let the children say goodbye.
My tribute to her years later.

# Love Your Memories - Anonymous

There are times when certain memories can only be captured in poetry like being anonymous and literally unseen in North London.

Selling plants all morning
One Saturday in May.
Months of work to grow
For our special charity day.

Any left were mentioned
In the local church on Sunday
And for those who wanted plants,
I'd be outside the church on Monday.

Two ladies did appear
And while the plants were packed,
We spoke of a mutual friend
And were glad that she'd come back.

At length one lady puzzled how
I'd seen our friend on Sunday,
And asked if I had been at church?
And this was only Monday.

I said I'd been the preacher,
(I was tickled to the core),
A moment, then she cried,
'That's where I've seen your face before.'

Who could not weep after hearing of this child…

# KNOWN ONLY AS 'P'

Seeing his innocent little face
Clinging to beg for crumbs of care
As though undeserved
Breaks my heart.

Who could fail to see the child-like
Love, trusting through the hard beating
Crucifying his little body,
Lest his little spirit break.

He is too small to question
The reasons for his plight,
His constancy tried over time while
He takes on himself our sins of cruelty.

Teaching us again our Lord's answer
To the evil of this world.

# MAGIC MOMENT

Come and look Mummy!
Little feet pattering to my side,
A child's hand in mine
Urging attention,
Pulling me to that patch of ground,
Breathless in wonder.
Little fingers pointing to
The tiny green shoot.
The first flower perhaps?
Too early yet to know
What lies beneath
This little thumbnail of promise
Stilled by the early dew.
Making us treasure this moment
In joy, of future hope in
One so young delighting in
Springtime come around.
And…

# Even the Sparrow

After so long working with the child
to help him understand.
To be calm and begin to turn outwards
dispensing with rough play
and form words that had meaning.
With music, repeated messages, pointing at things
Gaining his attention with unorthodox
yet not cruel means. The catalyst
showing utter response, knowing
where he was in the scheme of things.
Making him see life was not a game of whim
but a flesh and blood reality.

Then O bliss, the shop well known,
he uttered a clear, 'good morning;'
twice before it was taken up
by mother telling of the wonder
with crying joyful praise
at the miracle of his first words.

More Memories; There are some memories you just have to remember in this way to free the mind of all unhappy thoughts but know what happened.

# AND SO WE LIVE

I am just a child
Do you find me amusing?
With my broken teeth that give me
Pain when I test tea.
I am happy to be teased in such a fashion,
I laugh with you to keep you friendly.
My good neighbour.


My family never seem to notice
So I can be myself but know my
Limitations. Never to smile openly
Or laugh in photographs unless
I have checked my lip is covering
My dental impediment.


At school, children call me names
And follow me home, criss-crossing
The road as I try to avoid their taunts.
I don't laugh with them but pray that
One day they'll see me and stop
Their jeering and we can be friends.

To my shame, one day I did become
Sure I might stop their cruel ploys.
When almost home and trembling all over
I struck out at my tormentor and it was over,
Mother had been watching from a window
And was not amused, only seemed to frown
On my descent into less acceptable ways
Of dealing with trouble.


Soon I will have the problem fixed
And then I will smile and laugh
A little too much and let the hidden me
Out; and take delight in watching others
See the different me.

# Love Your Memories (Having Come So Far)

Some memories are so important to us that they are in fact part of ourselves, although we don't always recognise them as such at the time.

It was in the early 1990s, having struggled through the final stages of my ordination course, which really challenged me, in the best possible way. I felt close to my colleagues and hopefully respected by them, although not necessarily at one with, in certain aspects of service delivery, though, I personally embraced all our denominations, and felt privileged to have been accepted into what was, a predominately Anglican course.

The climax came when we were told we had fulfilled the necessary requirements to be ordained ministers of the church, and could obtain our ordination hood in due course.

It was well-known that there was an all-important vote about to take place as to whether women should be admitted to the Anglican priesthood. In the midst of all the soul-searching and fears that the result would once again dash the hopes of so many, there was great joy in hearing that the vote had gone in the women's favour.

I was fortunate that it was not an issue in my church. Women had long since been admitted to the ministry, but I could feel how it might be for many of my friends who had been through the course with me. There were great celebrations and ordination took on new meaning for all of us.

We all supported one another through the various ceremonies which brought us even closer in a Spiritual bond which in the end was what it was all about.

A special joy for me was being invited to preach in Dulwich College Chapel shortly after my ordination. I felt so respected and it greatly added to my feeling of closeness to my Anglican colleagues. The day included a walk through the magnificent Art Gallery with all its treasures being pointed out, then tea with my friend and finally being presented with a book full of the gallery's art collection. I felt like Royalty and the memory is as vivid as though it was yesterday. I cannot count the hours of extreme pleasure that book has given me and continues to bring back a very special moment in time.

# Love Your Memories - Francis Gay

When I was twelve, I was persuaded by my grandfather to send a poem I had written to Francis Gay of the Sunday Post. Living in Glasgow this seemed an exciting thing to do. I didn't know if I'd even get a reply, but back came a letter, which I read so often I began to know most of it by heart: it read thanking me first for sending it to him, then saying how sorry he was, not to be able to accept my poem, as he had already accepted more than he could print; then the letter continued; 'but go on writing poetry, and don't be downhearted that it is difficult to get into print, because one day you will see yourself in print, and know that your helpful and inspiring thoughts have reached others and have thus blessed them.'

Many years later, when I was now living in Dorset, and having continued to write poetry, with the name of Francis Gay still very much in vogue, sending encouragement and much needed comfort to so many. I decided to write to the Sunday Post, as the column was still being printed every Sunday under the same name, and with some encouragement from my cousin who had actually been present when Grandpa made his suggestion all those years ago.

I took the courage to write to whoever was now in charge, telling them my story. I received a wonderful letter, in reply, saying how pleased he, meaning Francis Gay himself, was to know of the inspiration that letter had given me. He said he felt heartened and humbled to know that those motivating words meant something to me. The letter ended by wishing me all the very best and hoping I had settled in well to my new life in Dorset. And of course signed,

Francis Gay

# Love Your Memories - Haggis

My first memory of being offered haggis was at a Burns Supper when I was seven. My sister and I had been taken to the supper to entertain, my sister Isobel to sing and I to recite some poetry.

We would not usually perform just after eating, but at the supper, the entertainment, apart from the formalities with the piping in of the haggis and someone rendering 'Address to the Haggis' as they cut into the haggis, which was then served to the waiting audience, with mashed potatoes and mashed swede and possibly some peas, if desired. We both declined to eat a portion after being given a spoonful to taste. My taste buds did not warm to it as it already seemed too hot and fiery, and certainly as I realised years later could not be enjoyed without the potato and Swedish Turnip, which when brought to Scotland became known as Scottish Turnip and then known in Scotland as swede, which is the original name of the plant when found in Sweden.

Many years later having become better acquainted with haggis, partly because my husband was fond of it around the twenty-fifth of January, I endeavoured to find the best one on the market. By this time we were living in Enfield, North London and haggis was not quite the favoured meal as in Scotland, and usually only appeared in specific butchers shops, who would advertise it in the window for those interested. I was passing one of those fine butchers one day around the time when haggis was sought after, and was delighted to see lots of haggises hanging up – Ah! That was the breaking point.

I went into the shop to inform the butcher, that haggis must never be hung. It is not an actual fowl, although a large part of what it consists of is fowl or animal related. If it is pierced before being boiled, it will simply burst and float out into the boiling water. Not a pretty sight.

Around this time I happened to be teaching a group on public speaking in Further Education. Hearing I was going to Scotland for a short time, in the early New Year, a number of them asked if I would bring them back a haggis; only one of the group was Scottish and I don't quite remember how the subject came up. Most had never tasted haggis, and one or two didn't know what it was, so an interesting conversation followed, and I did promise to do my best to bring back some haggises.

On arriving in Glasgow, I knew my family would know the best butcher to go to if you wanted haggis. One butcher in particular was thought to be the best producer of haggis. So after some family time, I was ready to purchase the haggises to take back with me to Enfield. I don't quite remember what happened when I went through Customs, with one case noticeably heavier and when opened revealing a number of haggises, each around a pound in weight, comfortably housed across the top. They were still fresh when the group started again, and there was some excitement when the haggises were offered, of course with strict instructions as to cooking and the must serve with accompaniments.

One of the tastiest haggises I have had was a tinned one, by a well-known maker. Easy to cook and serve with no spillages.

# The Car-Park Incident

Yesterday, I was trying to manoeuvre my car out of a space in our local car park with two hefty cars, one on either side of me and a car parked right behind me with two of its wheels on the grass verge, leaving little space for me to get out.

After several attempts with the sensors going at every turn, I sat there for some time looking for someone returning to their car, to ask for help.

At last someone came near enough to ask. I called out and he came over. He was happy to help and proceeded to give me signals, but because the sensors were constantly indicating 'stop' I was unable to continue. In the end the young man very kindly offered to get the car out for me. I gladly accepted and was so relieved.

It took many turns and twists during which time even he became anxious, and when eventually he succeeded in getting the car clear, with a few near misses, there was great relief on both sides.

I thanked him profusely, and as I said, he had also found it very scary and made a point of adding that I was right to be scared.

My confidence was restored.
Written on 12th November, 2019

# THE GIFT

It's not bought with the pounds in your pocket.
Though it helps to have a few.
It's not all the qualifications
Or the number of things you do.

In a moment of seclusion,
Hardly breathing, fixed and calm,
As our mind sifts through the stillness
And shuts out noise and harm.

Driven on in seconds
Before you count to ten,
Broken in a moment
By the need to think again.

For all the love we've witnessed,
Things drifting from the past
Together bound with present day
We seek some peace at last.

Let past and present be justified,
Though each has taken its toll;
By means of grace we triumph
When forgiveness floods the soul.